From

WHEELCHAIR

to

PLAYGROUND

My Faith Goal

MARCIA A. HUGHES

ISBN 978-1-0980-3572-3 (paperback)
ISBN 978-1-0980-3573-0 (digital)

Christian Faith Publishing, Inc.
832 Park Avenue
Meadville, PA 16335
www.christianfaithpublishing.com

Printed in the United States of America

To my parents for laying a strong Christian foundation in my life, though they are now in heaven; I thank them for their unconditional love, support, and for always being there for me.

Parents & Haley

CONTENTS

Acknowledgments 7

Foreword 9

Prologue 11

Chapter 1: Ever Seen a Grown Man Cry?....................................13

Chapter 2: It's a Girl 16

Chapter 3: The Early Days 21

Chapter 4: Love Thy Neighbor 23

Chapter 5: Eyes to See..28

Chapter 6: Renewal of Faith 34

Chapter 7: Wally...38

Chapter 8: An Attack 42

Chapter 9: To Playground..49

Chapter 10: The Healing Process 55

Epilogue 63

A Note to the Reader..71

A Letter from Heaven..78

ACKNOWLEDGMENTS

My deepest gratitude goes to:
My heavenly Father who guided my hand on every page of this book and who chose me to be Haley's mom.

Thank you to my husband, Wally, for unselfishly taking a chance on Haley and making our lives his priority. He walked in and accepted Haley as his own. I love you so much!

To my brother, Steve, who stood by me and was a surrogate "dad" for Haley.

To my boss, Tom, and the LGI Land family I worked with over the years for their love and support. They encouraged me to write this book. I love and miss you all!

A huge thank-you goes to Haley's teachers (especially Karla). I love the cute little *art* projects you sent home with her. I cherish the handprint crafts you all made for us parents. Those *little* things are *huge* when your child is gone. I thank you all so much.

A huge thank-you and hug for my fun and loving sister-in-law, who spent many hours turning a big, handwritten notebook with scattered notes into an organized book that I'll cherish forever.

FOREWORD

Marcia and I were very fortunate to grow up with strong Christian parents and a strong work ethic by growing up on a farm.

While we were growing up, we fought like cats and dogs, but always had each other's back against outsiders. After high school, we became very close.

Both our lives have been a roller coaster of financial and personal highs and lows. At one of the lowest part of my life, Marcia invited me to live with her. Looking back now I feel strongly that was God's will. She was there for me at a difficult time in my life and I was able to be with her during Haley's birth and to help when Haley got out of the hospital. It was a crushing time for Marcia. She almost lost her own life and had to face Haley's horrible disabilities. At first it seemed like a horrible blow, but as time went on, Haley's disabilities strengthened and enriched both our lives.

This book is a shining example of loss and victory. You will shed tears of sorrow and of joy.

I'm extremely proud of my sister for creating such an amazing and uplifting book. The hand of God was definitely guiding her.

Steve Hadley, brother of Marcia

This book is about unconditional love, goals, and God. Marcia's belief in God and goals gave her the courage to face all of the challenges of Haley's health. She explains this through the use of scriptures from the Bible. The book is sad but can be uplifting at the same time. I would recommend everyone read this book, especially anyone who is in a similar circumstance.

—Thomas E. Lipar (Founder of LGI Land and LGI Homes)

Wow, just wow! Sweet Marcia, as I was reading your words through tear-filled eyes and heart-tugging smiles; I have never felt so comfortable with my faith. As long as I've known you, your faith has been such a strong part of who you are. I can remember many, many times you used it to redirect me! Even after knowing you these past nineteen years, I feel as though we have just been introduced in a brand-new way. I can only hope one day to be the faithful believer you are. You have opened your heart and exposed your most sacred inner feelings in a way that will inspire everyone reading Haley's story to strive to be a better person. I am humbled and beyond grateful to call you my friend.

—Karen Brooks (Friend and former boss at LGI Land)

From Wheelchair to Playground is a captivating love story of a mother and her daughter, Haley. This story chronicles the life events of caring for a special needs child; and a mother who loved, and stood in prayer for her healing.

While God had another plan, this true story takes you through both good and difficult times, and although Haley's life on this earth ended; it shows us how God brought this family through a grief process, and ultimately brought inner healing to all.

This book is an outstanding testimony of God's love; and a look at life, death, grief, loss, faith, hope, love, and healing.

Anyone who has loved and lost a child, or had a loss of any kind, will find renewed strength and healing in Jesus, by reading this.

I highly recommend this book.

—Cathy Jenkins (Friend, and Health Care Provider)

PROLOGUE

On September 17, 2003, I attended a sales training at work. Sales professionals become successful by setting and accomplishing sets of goals. In my field, goals are broken into monthly, annual, multi-year, and lifetime goals. That day, the first part of our training included time to write a lifetime goal, unrelated to work, that would be given to the president of our company so he could encourage us to accomplish it. We were asked to submit our plan to him within thirty days. I decided then that writing this book would be my goal. At the time, I really didn't know what writing it would take or what the end product would be. I knew declaring it as a book made me very nervous, but it also felt important that I complete it. A few weeks later, I typed my plan to compose my manuscript and mailed it off to the president of the company.

This book is about the life of my daughter, Haley Elizabeth. Even now, years after she has gone to be with Jesus, I have moments when I wish she was still in my tummy, actively kicking, before delivery. At that time, my goal had been to have a natural childbirth. I had even hired a birth coach to help me have the most perfect birth imaginable. Visualization is a sales-goal technique I was taught in my professional life, and I applied that practice to envision a successful birth. I was determined to be prepared; I read books and watched videos constantly to make sure I was fully prepared for labor. I felt certain I could accomplish my goal.

When I visualized giving birth, I imagined the birth coach cheering me on and the doctor announcing I had delivered a healthy baby girl. I imagined a beautiful newborn laid on my tummy for that first bonding as mother and daughter. I imagined introducing myself to with the words, "I'm your mommy, Haley Elizabeth." I imagined all smiles, joy, congratulations, and celebration of new life. But my visualizations never came to pass.

My joy—and my daughter—were taken away from me at two thirty in the morning after an emergency cesarean. Due to trauma we both experienced in the birth, I never got to hold Haley after she was born. While I was barely conscious, she was whisked away to another hospital for specialized treatment for the unforeseen condition she suffered in the womb.

It would have been easy, normal even, to be discouraged by the sense that I had not accomplished my goal. But God, in his infinite grace, chose other plans. The first was to take Haley and me on a journey of discovery about healing. The second was to redefine my goals around his will for our lives.

The goal of Haley's life was to bring glory to God. She accomplished that goal just by being Haley. Through her interactions with her family, teachers, and friends, hers was a life that illuminated glory of God. I was privileged to see it all from beginning to end. My life goal—and yours as well, I might add—is exactly the same, only accomplished in other ways. I believe that finishing this book is one step toward my life goal, and my prayer is that the glory of God would shine brightly through it in the same way it did through Haley's life.

And now, let us start at the beginning.

CHAPTER 1

Ever Seen a Grown Man Cry?

I had been experiencing terrible indigestion for nearly a month. Heartburn this bad can accompany a gallstone, I thought. Mom had one once. The doctor recommended an ultrasound and, sure enough, he found a small gallstone. He recommended surgery and scheduled it two weeks out, just after his return from vacation.

During the weeks of waiting, new symptoms emerged. One morning, while driving to work, I got sick on the side of the road (of course, it would have to be right in the middle of town!) When I got to work, I told a coworker about the experience. When she asked me whether I might be pregnant, I scoffed at the idea. I had been married before and, never having gotten pregnant then, doubted it would ever happen.

After a few more trips to the bathroom throughout the morning, I decided to humor myself. I stopped by the drugstore after work and bought a home pregnancy test. If you've never taken a pregnancy test before, it's important to know the dot turn pinks to indicate a positive result. And that's exactly what happened when I took it. Thinking of my recent gallstone diagnosis, I dialed the pregnancy test company in a panic; surely, I thought, other factors could trigger a false positive. When no one answered the line, I went back to the drugstore to buy another test brand, convinced this test would yield a different outcome. But no, I got another positive result! Convinced that the presence of a gallstone was affecting my test results, I decided to make an appointment with my gynecologist.

An ultrasound revealed I was definitely ten weeks and three days pregnant. The situation was ironic: I had wanted children for years but, due to a battle with endometriosis, was under the impression that I couldn't conceive (short of immaculate conception!). This time, my circumstances were less than ideal. Pregnant for the first time at forty-five years old, the news was a shock to me and my family. When I shared the news with my parents and siblings, their pause indicated they were waiting for a punch line. When they realized I wasn't joking, the response was excitement and happiness all around. That is, everyone except for one person.

I met Haley's dad, a good-looking guy in a cowboy hat, one night while country western dancing. He asked me to dance. After learning that we had a lot in common (we both had a similar Christian background and were both in sales), our relationship took off. We had been dating for nearly two years when I found out I was pregnant. I didn't know how to tell him, and thinking about sharing the news made me a nervous wreck.

The evening after I visited the gynecologist, I headed to his place with dinner and a copy of the ultrasound.

"I have something to show you," I announced.

I placed a black-and-white ultrasound of our baby, arms and legs positioned as though paused in the middle of a jumping jack, in front of him on the table.

"This is your baby," I told him.

Silence. Finally, the words spilled out of his mouth, "How did this happen?"

Unlike my family, his emotions never did turn to joy. After two weeks of uncertainty, he decided he was definitely "not happy," and began to pull away. Over time, our relationship dwindled, until we were no longer in contact. I prayed for a change of heart, but lonely nights brought reality into focus: I was alone.

I didn't want everyone at work to know the sex of the baby yet, so I decided to wait a few weeks away for Christmas and give them something that would spill the beans. I decided on, along with their gift in each bag, to include a pink bubble gum cigar. A few of them pulled it out with a puzzled look on their face, and then one of them got it and yelled, "It's a girl!" They all started cheering and yelling. That was fun!

In the months ahead, I thought about what I wanted for the baby growing inside of me. I worried, like all single parents do, how I would help my child succeed and about what I wanted for them. One fear was "Can I really get this kid through school?" I'm lousy at school projects! My math skills suck, but I could, however, confidently claim that he or she would not complete a sentence with a double negative or end a sentence with a preposition! English was my thing. Then I thought maybe when the project time rolls around, I'll be married or have very resourceful neighbors!

One thing was certain: I wanted my child to grow up in a house with a yard in a nice neighborhood. So I began the house hunt. Hours of driving around neighborhoods turned to days spent searching for a home for my baby. I struggled to find more than a postage stamp lot in a price range I could afford until a friend from the gym suggested I look in her neighborhood. I quickly found a nice single family home with a fenced-in yard. After negotiations were complete, I was given a move-in date of April 1.

Two months before I closed on my house, I was put on bed rest. Unable to pack my own belongings, my parents, brother, and friends chipped in to pack my three-bedroom apartment and moved me into my new home on the other side of town. Forbidden by my doctor to walk, my two kitties and I were the last things my friends and family carted out the door!

CHAPTER 2

It's a Girl

As my due date approached, I became increasingly, though unsurprisingly, more uncomfortable. My doctor took me off terbutaline, an intravenous prescription drug required throughout my bed rest, and finally allowed me to go out for short walks. My mom and I took advantage of my new liberties with an outing to the Baby Superstore. After years of buying baby gifts for others, it was fun to shop for my own baby! Kroger, which was next door to the baby store, even let me borrow a motorized grocery cart to zip around the aisles!

My doctor had explained that most women go into labor within a couple of days of being taken off the terbutaline IV. At that time, I was thirty-six weeks pregnant and was experiencing regular contractions, but I still hadn't gone into labor. On April 24, my mom's birthday, and April 26, my nephew's birthday, I made an effort to kick start labor, but to no avail. On the 26th, I had a doctor's appointment and mentioned to the nurse that my side was really hurting. Not knowing what was considered normal at the end of pregnancy, I didn't press her to communicate more thoroughly with the doctor. In retrospect, I wish I had mentioned that pain to the doctor!

On the morning of Saturday, April 29, I woke up exhausted. Depleted of all energy and in pain, no matter what position I was in, I told my mom I couldn't do anything. She assured me that I would get a surge of energy prior to labor that would give me the strength to give birth. Unconvinced, and increasingly in pain, I suggested we call the doctor. Even so, I didn't call. Not long after, I felt my body begin to shut down. I hung my head, unable to open my eyes. I began sweating profusely. Finally, I asked my mother to call my child birth coach. When she answered we learned that Sally was on a house call. She said she would be leaving there shortly and would come right over.

Within an hour, Sally arrived at my house. She checked my stomach for the baby's heartbeat and asked me when I last felt her moving around. I couldn't remember, and her question scared me. I could tell she was trying to stay calm, but I also recognized urgency in her voice. She phoned the doctor for me and found she wasn't on call that weekend but just happened to be there and would wait for us.

"Can you walk to the car?" Sally asked.

"No," I replied. She immediately called for an ambulance.

The ambulance seemed to take forever to arrive. They got lost on the way. The transition to the stretcher and ambulance was very painful. Sally rode with me in the ambulance, and every so often, I could hear her say, "Stay with us, Marcia." Her voice was constant and reassuring.

We met my doctor in the emergency room; she looked worried. They rushed me into an operating room; my stomach was so hard, the doctor thought I must be having contractions. After a quick exam, she noted in a panicked voice, "She's not dilated."

Nurses and doctors swirled around me. Suddenly, I felt a warm solution flow over my stomach along with the insertion of an IV, and then I was out.

*****

I wasn't aware that anything had happened until I heard a gentle voice say, "You had a girl."

I tried to open my eyes slightly. I realized I was in a recovery room, but I couldn't fully awaken. My next conscious moment came hours later, around two thirty in the morning. Barely conscious, I was told my daughter was experiencing some medical problems and needed to be transported to Texas Children's Hospital.

"Do you want to see her first?" the nurse asked. Of course, I did!

Surrounded by my family, I saw my chubby little girl with long dark hair. *Is that hair what caused all my indigestion?* All I could do was reach through the little hole in her incubator to touch her briefly before she was whisked away.

My own medical situation posed its own challenges. In rare moments of clarity, I learned that I had experienced an artery rupture. I woke up on Sunday afternoon, opened my eyes a bit, and noticed my brother with his head resting on his arms. Too exhausted to say anything, I drifted back into dreamland. A few hours later, a nurse came in my room.

"We're moving you from the ICU, but first I need to remove a tube in your nose," she said. "I want you to hold your breath and count to ten."

Let me tell you, if I had known what was about to happen, I would have stopped her. She pulled what seemed to be fifty feet of tubing out of my nose. Wow, that hurt!

"We've given you nearly five units of blood," she told me. "You're lucky to be alive."

No one mentioned anything about my baby girl, and I was too sick to ask.

A few days later, my doctor began to fit the puzzle pieces together to help me make sense of my situation. When she began speaking, she broke down in tears. She explained that when she found the ruptured artery, she stitched it too close to the tube that ran from my kidneys to my bladder. Accidentally, she had closed off the tube, which meant I wasn't expelling the fluids my body needed to release. After consulting with a urologist, she was confirmed that, without additional surgery to place a stent, I wouldn't survive.

At Texas Children's Hospital (TCH), my family had stepped into the full-time role of caring for a brand-new baby girl named Haley Elizabeth. I longed to be with her, but after two surgeries, I was limited to recovery in the maternity ward. One day the phone rang, and it was one of Haley's doctors. I asked him about Haley's condition, but he consistently dodged my questions, assuring me that he would explain the details when I was able to come to the hospital in person. His approach really bothered me. It felt as though no one would give me any information.

Finally, I was given the green light to go on temporary "leave" from the hospital so I could visit Haley. I was still very weak and had a lot of stomach discomfort, but I was determined to see my baby. If you could have seen me, you might have thought that I looked like the "Pillsbury dough girl!" I was swollen from my head to the end of my toes. I couldn't even wear shoes!

When I finally got to the NIC-U, my parents both wanted to see me hold Haley for the first time. Since only two adults were allowed in the NIC-U at once, my mom graciously gave my dad the honors. I walked in and saw tiny preemies, some only a couple of pounds, everywhere. And then there was Haley! She was big and beautiful. Her long dark hair was gone, shaved off for IV's; only one little tuft of sideburn and a little bit on the top of her forehead remained. Like any mother would, I inspected that kid from one end to the other! She had all her fingers and toes. She didn't look like the same chubby baby I had met at two thirty in the morning. Her features were like a little porcelain doll, and her eyelashes seemed to stretch for miles. She was absolutely perfect.

When it was time to meet with Haley's medical team, I sat with a group of neurologists around a big intimidating table. They broke the news to me that my perfect baby wasn't perfect. She had suffered a great loss of oxygen due to my artery aneurysm, which led to irreversible brain damage. The front part of her brain, which controls motor skills, had taken the brunt of the damage. The doctor began listing off the functions her body wouldn't be able to perform.

"She won't sit. She won't crawl. She won't walk, talk," they began.

I don't think I heard anything after that. I don't remember them saying she wouldn't see; I learned that at a later date. When I finally zoned back to reality, I heard one of the doctors ask, "Do you have any questions?"

I said, "No." I didn't know what to ask; I felt brain-dead.

Later that day, I went back to the hospital where I was a patient. To cope with the shock, my brain pushed everything I had heard deep into my memory bank until the experience seemed more like a dream than reality. On Saturday, Haley and I were both released. My parents and I headed down to Texas Children's Hospital. I picked out a cute little outfit for her to wear, and we headed for home.

CHAPTER 3

The Early Days

The Sunday after Haley and I were released from the hospital was Mother's Day. I had waited for years to celebrate that! My parents were still with us, since my body had not fully recovered from the trauma. Haley had been throwing up for a few days, and the soft spot on her head was bulging. We retreated to the hospital, only to receive no explanation for her symptoms other than more of her brain cells had died. That was my first Mother's Day.

I began calling friends and family for prayer and included Haley's father's parents in the phone tree. In response, they shared the news with their pastor, who immediately left Louisiana for Houston with another deacon to pray over Haley in the hospital and anoint her with oil for healing. From that day on, my mind could not accept any reality but one in which Haley would be totally healed.

One evening, a friend and I took Haley to Lakewood Church for midweek Bible study. I dressed her in an adorable blue-and-white nautical dress. During the service, Dodie Osteen called for anyone who had a need to come to the front for prayer. I took Haley up to her and explained our situation. She thought she was adorable and told me that her daughter was diagnosed with cerebral palsy when she was young, but that God had healed her through praying healing scriptures over her every day! I have heard her share that testimony many times, so I pictured myself doing the very same thing with

Haley. She provided me with the healing scriptures, and I started to read them over her daily.

Even as a baby, Haley had a cute personality. My parents bought her a toddler recliner and we would frequently put her in it and lean her back. One day she made a face by moving her eyes to one side and making a big frown. I started to laugh, and she immediately grinned. From then on, she would make this face when she wanted to make us laugh. I was so glad to see she had a sense of humor like her mom! At bath time I would tickle her and she would laugh and laugh. I loved hearing that sound. I began to imagine Haley fully healed. Many people thought that I was in denial of her prognosis, but that didn't bother me. Either my faith was strong, or I was just stubborn; either way I decided to stand firm in my trust of God for Haley's future.

CHAPTER 4

Love Thy Neighbor

When the doctors first told me what to expect with Haley's development, I didn't have the capacity to realize the whole picture. I didn't think about follow-up appointments, financial implications, or sleep deprivation; it was as though my mind couldn't handle it. Slowly, I began feeling the weight of this new reality. Neither Haley nor I were spared from the load.

Haley's prognosis had extensive implications that I never could have imagined. In the early days, for example, I didn't think about taking her to the dentist. Because of all the medicines Haley was prescribed, her teeth started to rot and break off. During her dental checkups, the dentist would tell us she needed fillings and caps for her teeth, which meant frequent trips to Texas Children's Hospital for surgical procedures to cap her teeth. The procedures cost thousands of dollars, and we didn't have dental insurance, but surgical procedures were covered under medical insurance. This was just the beginning of God's provision for us in times of need.

Haley suffered other complications from the trauma of her birth. Her involuntary back arching, twisting and wrenching of her body caused one of her legs to grow nearly two inches longer than the other and caused her hip joints to dislocate. She eventually underwent a procedure to cut her leg extender muscles to prevent them from getting too tight, but I wasn't sure what to do about her hip dislocation. A doctor suggested a procedure to cut her femur and hip bones and fuse a piece of her leg to her hip socket to create a *C* instead of an open *L* in her hip joint. He told me the surgery would be painful and her leg would be permanently shortened. I was distraught by the idea of the surgery and asked God for guidance. As I walked out of his office that day, the thought immediately hit my mind, "Jesus's bones were never broken." I felt that was my answer. Her bones won't be broken either, I thought to myself.

Haley's complications didn't stop there. Issues that are simple for most bodies to manage, like allergies, caused great problems for her. For example, when her sinuses would drain, her muscles were too weak to help her swallow appropriately, so she would need constant attention and suctioning to help her manage her saliva. Eating and drinking was another challenge; she could only handle a tiny spoonful of food or water at a time. I would cook her food, blend it, and thicken it with baby rice cereal to create a consistency that wouldn't choke her. She loved pumpkin pie filling. It would take several attempts to clear her throat and swallow the food or water she was given. Beyond that, she needed a total of six breathing treatments just to help her during allergy season.

She needed hand braces to keep her hands from curling, feet braces to straighten crooked feet, and leg braces to help her legs grow properly. All the while, her seizures continued. Once in a while she received shots in her neck, arms, and hands to relax her tightened muscles. Whereas most new parents experience frequent visits to the pediatrician, we saw the full gamut of medical professionals on a regular basis: allergist, neurologists, dentists, orthopedists, dietitians, and more.

The load was, at times, unbearable. But the hardest part was not the attention she needed, it was when she cried. I never knew where she hurt or what to treat. Without God, the weight of our needs would have crushed me. And in the beginning, as a single parent, there were so many things that took my attention away from him or caused me to direct negative attention to him. The endless competing demands for my time from doctor's appointments, phone calls, household errands, and grocery shopping, not to mention the pressure of a commission-only sales job, placed stress on every moment of my life. In the chaos that surrounded us, I often felt like I had little time to devote to God. Luckily, God always had time for us, and he was looking out for us all along.

There were a lot of issues to deal with regarding different nannies I had for my daughter. Sometimes I let them run my life. I didn't like it, but I allowed it because I had a lot on my plate. People told me I let some of them take advantage of me, and I did, but the fight or conflict wasn't worth it. My mind-set was, I'm dealing every day with the urgent things and anything less can be put aside. There was financial stress when my mind was on my circumstances too much and my joy just wasn't there. I don't think I really laughed for a whole year one time. There was one night I can look back and laugh at now, but at that time it was another stress.

One evening when Haley was in her "throwing-up" stage, my cat, Savannah, came up next to us. Haley hit the cat with one of her projectiles in perfect precision! A vomit-soaked cat went running all through the house. Haley was also covered from head to toe. I laid her on the floor and went outside to seek help. New to the neighborhood, I didn't know anyone very well. I knocked on the next-door neighbor's house and told her my dilemma. Being a cat lover, she came to the rescue, gathered up Savannah, and gave her a bath while I gave Haley one. God had surely directed us to the right neighborhood!

I wasn't the only mom to Haley, it turns out. My kitty, Savannah, had a natural instinct to "mother." She took it upon herself to bring little varmints into the house like geckos and put them under where Haley would sit in an attempt to feed her! I couldn't yell at her. She was so attentive to everything she did. She wanted to sleep under her crib at night. She loved Haley so much.

One day my friend Kari was giving Haley a bath in the tub upstairs and Haley was crying. Savannah came running upstairs into the bathroom to see what was wrong with "our" little girl. Kari said Savannah peeked over the edge of the tub. After Kari brought Haley downstairs, wrapped in a towel, Savannah jumped up beside her and started consoling her by patting her with her paw as if to say, "It's okay, Haley." I just had to share that.

I later found out Haley was allergic to cats and had to set Savannah up in the garage. It was traumatic for her because she didn't understand as she had always been inside the house for thirteen years. She was soon killed by a dog in our front yard. (She never left the premises.) The devastation was a close second to losing a child.

When God led me to our neighborhood before Haley was born, I didn't know the school district was one of the best in the nation for children with special needs. Geared for kids ages three to nineteen years old, the school system was a God-send for Haley and me. The day after she turned three, Haley was loaded in her tiny wheelchair onto the bus and off to school. My older brother from Oklahoma and my parents were in town for her third birthday; together, all of us saw her off for her first day of school. We all stood at the end of the driveway and bawled as the bus went down the street! It could have been a viral YouTube video.

As it turns out, the teachers were wonderful. They helped set goals for Haley, like learning to reach intentionally for an object. There was an art class for textures, a cooking class for foods and tastes, unique switches to touch that would turn on music for the children and more. The teachers were kept busy with feedings and diaper changes too. Haley was one of the few children fed by mouth. When report card time came around, I would see the same goals and objectives, every quarter, every year. I had a sick feeling in the pit of my stomach, but I still believed she would be healed! To me, it was just the matter of when.

The presence of the school was an indication of God's divine provision for us; they embodied what it means to love thy neighbor. As a parent with a child of special needs, it helped to have other adults who understood our situation. I've encountered so many people who think they're dumb or stare at them because they're uncomfortable. As a parent, that was heartbreaking. But Haley loved people, despite how they treated her. She loved the kids in the neighborhood, so I made sure they came to visit her so she would be stimulated by their company. At times, I would hear people say, "I couldn't do what you do, why don't you take her somewhere?" But that thought had never crossed my mind; as challenging as our situation was, I loved her more than anything and delighted in being her mom.

There was a season of Haley's life, which lasted nearly a year, when she cried day and night. During that time, she would look at me as though to say, "Why can't you help me?" I almost lost it. Attempts to consult with the doctor would result in prescriptions, often the medications we had tried before. I had to work a lot of hours and couldn't get any sleep. During that time, a good friend and former neighbor offered to come to our house one night a week so I could sleep. Kari was a God-send.

Still, Haley's crying persisted. At some point, I heard about kinesiology and acupuncture with touch, which I learned can work wonders to identify the root cause of chronic problems in children. I did some research to find a professional in this field who could care for Haley's needs and found that, while one doctor was in Florida, the other was less than a mile from our house! What a miracle!

After our first appointment, the doctor told me, "This baby has been having horrible headaches!" After one session, in which he adjusted parts of her face and the roof of her mouth, we went home and she slept soundly through the night! After that day, I rarely needed to wake up with her in the middle of the night. What a blessing! I praised the Lord for this answer to prayer, just up the street!

CHAPTER 5

Eyes to See

As he went along, he saw a man blind from birth.
His disciples asked him, "Rabbi, who sinned, this
man or his parents, that he was born blind?"

—John 9:1–2

In the story of Jesus healing the blind man, the disciples asked Jesus who had sinned, the man or his parents, to cause the man to be born blind. The story is ancient, but I relate with the sentiment. The question of the disciples is one of the first ones I had when I learned Haley wouldn't develop normally. Was God punishing me for my past sin? Furthermore, I wasn't married when I conceived Haley, and because of that sin, I was afraid God would hold it against me by withholding his healing. None of this seemed fair, however; Haley was innocent.

Few people look at a handicapped child and ask, "I wonder what great works will be accomplished by God through this child." But why do we assume nothing good can come from a child with disabilities? I have come to believe that this way of thinking is an abomination. Every child is created in the image of God; no one is worthless and no one is a mistake. God uses all people to accomplish his purposes.

Unfortunately, I encountered too many people who missed the opportunity to see God's glory working in and through Haley. Many of them, sadly, were her caregivers. As the demands for Haley's care grew, I hired a live-in nanny to assist me with her need. She understood, but did not speak, English, but I decided to take a chance on her nonetheless. Not long after she started, my mom (who was still visiting) noticed that eggs were quickly disappearing from our refrigerator. One day, I glanced under Haley's portable crib we had downstairs and noticed a raw egg in a bowl under there. Not long after, my mom caught the nanny holding Haley upside down and hitting the bottom of her feet. I, of course, immediately fired the nanny. It turned out that she was a highly superstitious person and was supposedly attempting, according to her belief, to drive evil spirits out of Haley. Instead of recognizing the glory of God in her and treating her with love, the nanny used demonic superstitious spirits and mistreated her in the process.

After that experience, I hired another woman who had raised five children of her own. I knew she was older, but I never knew her exact age. A former lounge singer, she still had a lovely voice and sang to Haley often. She was a colorful woman with amazing stories. One day while I was at the gym, I received a phone call from her. In hysterics, she told me that a jet plane had flown over our home, something had fallen off the plane, and had landed in my backyard. She insisted we notify the airport immediately because she was certain the plane might crash. She told me it looked like part of an engine. We were on the flight path from the airport, so, odd as it seemed, the story was plausible. When I got home she had already called 911. An officer came and looked at what had allegedly fallen off the plane. Out in the yard was laying the circular attic fan that has fallen and rolled off of my roof. I was so embarrassed! I later found out that she had lied about her age to get the job and was actually eighty years old!

The next time I hired a caregiver, I had the awful experience of receiving a call at work from the police. Haley's nanny had run in the store for a brief moment to pick up something but had left Haley asleep in her car seat. A passerby called the police and an ambulance to make sure Haley hadn't passed out. Haley was fine, but the experience was awful.

One lady I hired and things seemed to go smoothly. Then one day she cried and said she missed her little dog so much and could she bring her to my house. I hired live-ins due to my work schedule. I was exhausted from work and didn't need any added stress. I went upstairs to change and had "words" with God. I started whining to him, "Lord," I said, "I don't want a dog here in my house. It will pee and chew up stuff; I just can't have a dog in my house!" And I got the shock of my life when I heard an audible voice say, "This is not your house, it's mine! It's yours to live in while you are on this earth, but it's mine!" Whoa! The first time in my life I've heard God actually speak to me like he's standing next to me, and he chewed me out. So, yes, I told her the dog could come. Luckily it wasn't a yippy one, but it wasn't long after that I had four chair legs chewed and puppies running around.

Just remember, when after school day cares don't work and you need an in-home caregiver, you bring their problems into your home also.

I absolutely loved a precious lady named Betty from Trinidad. She and I are still in touch. She was with me a year, only supposed to be in the states six months, but we couldn't stand to part.

The challenges of our lifestyle pressed against us at every side. Seemingly little things, like not having enough time to go to the gym, weighed on me. Before Haley was born, I was at the gym from four to six hours a week to help with mental stress. After she was born, I had no time and no outlet to release my frustrations. I felt trapped and, at times, it seemed that I had no life apart from bearing the heavy demands of her disability. I blamed her and, sometimes, blamed God as well. A love-hate relationship developed. I loved my daughter but hated my circumstances. I didn't like myself anymore. I got too serious about life, because my life was serious.

Miss Betty and Haley

Over the next five years, more caregivers came in and out of our lives. One, Edna, had a positive impact on us. I hired her when I was still in the why-did-this-happen stage of my life journey. I quickly noted that Edna spent a lot of time reading her Bible, something that I admired but was always too exhausted to do. One morning I sat down with her.

"Where should I start reading?" I asked her.

Edna said, "Pray for wisdom and start reading Proverbs."

I prayed for wisdom and understanding, and the Lord began to open up the Scriptures to me as never before! I had read the Bible a lot in my life, but I began reading things that I had never before noticed. Reading Scripture began to change my way of thinking. I began to see the power we have in Christ, the gifts of the Holy Spirit, and the love of the Father in ways I previously had not understood. I also noticed that Satan was constantly putting thoughts of defeat, fear, hopelessness, and victimhood in my mind. I made a commitment that I would not allow him to control my thoughts any longer.

I also had to change another habit. I said to myself, "The power of life and death is in my mouth! What I say is what I get." I read in Isaiah 53:5, "He was wounded for our transgressions. He was bruised for our iniquities. The chastisement for our peace was upon Him, and by His stripes we were healed." He (Jesus) said we were healed. I had always believed that Haley had already received her healing but did not always speak it.

I was spending so much time talking about Haley's inadequacies from cerebral palsy, I was missing the bigger picture. Jesus died for Haley and, regardless of my sin or our circumstances, would never withhold his healing power from her. If the power of life and death is in the tongue (Proverbs 18:21), I knew I needed to begin to acknowledge verbally that his healing was for her. At bedtime, I began saying, "Who healed you, Haley? Jesus did!" Haley was healed by Jesus's stripes.

I've been told that God gives *special* children to special people. It was hard for me to understand that in my early days of motherhood. There was even a time when I really believed God was punishing me with a seemingly unbearable situation. In reality, it was quite the contrary. Looking back and knowing what I do now, would I have traded her for a perfectly normal child? Absolutely not. Through Haley, God gave me the opportunity to expand my faith, experience unconditional love, be filled with joy, and draw closer to Him.

Not only me, but I saw Haley bring immense joy to her grandparents, who loved getting to hold her, feed her, and feel needed in their later years. Haley especially loved to lay in Grandpa's lap for hours on end. How many grandchildren would do that? She also brought such joy to her teachers and others in our neighborhood.

Children with unique needs, like Haley, touch the lives of people around them every day. Those who have the chance to be around them see the gifts they are to others. If we allow God to remove our blindness, we will see God work mightily through these precious souls. They are not worthless to society. God can and will create mighty works through their lives (Philippians 2:6). Haley was a blessing to so many people and, over time, the blessings just kept coming and coming.

CHAPTER 6

Renewal of Faith

It wasn't hard to believe that Haley was a blessing, but it did take time to move beyond the pain, anger, disappointment, and stress of why life turned out the way it did for us. I often heard the phrase "All things work out for good," but being left to deal with the reality of suffering made it hard to embrace that concept. It takes faith, stamina, patience, and the will to survive to not surrender to the temptation and give up.

How in the world can a woman with a severe lack of self-esteem believe that God would answer her prayer with such a mighty miracle that her family and friends would fall on their knees and worship the living God? It begins with caring people. I once heard a sermon at her grandparents' church on how to make a difference in a person's life from a biblical perspective. If we consider the account in Scripture of the blind man who sought Jesus for healing by following him home or the story of the lame man who had to be lowered through the roof on a stretcher to reach Jesus below, we are forced to consider the caring people who brought them before the Healer.

I found out one day that a group of loving men of faith, men who we didn't even know, were lifting us before the Healer in prayer. Because of the prayers of men in a prison ministry, I made it through bouts of severe depression and found the strength to endure. Their prayers for us enabled me to care well for Haley and develop the fortitude to hold on in times of distress.

The support of prayer from people who did not know us, not only in the prison ministry but in the many other churches who rallied around us in prayer during seasons of trial, taught me a lot about standing firm in faith and learning to forgive. Ultimately, it compelled me to examine my thoughts and my words. In the early years of Haley's life, I began to learn that the enemy takes great delight in diverting our attention from others so we focus solely on ourselves. I had struggled for years with low self-esteem. I wasn't married when I conceived Haley, and because of that sin, I felt God would hold it against me and withhold his healing from her. In another part, it had to do with self-confidence. (I couldn't even have a baby right.) Self-forgiveness felt impossible, maybe because I felt like I didn't deserve it.

One day, my boss came into my office and told me, "God told me to tell you that what happened with Haley wasn't because of any past sin of yours." That brought healing to my soul. Jesus answered the disciples' question in John 9:3, "Neither this man nor his parents sinned, but that the works of God should be revealed in him." He healed that man's blindness that day.

In that season, I was reminded that God said, "As far as the East is from the West, that is how far the transgressions are between us" (Psalm 103:12). We can't pick and choose the scriptures that we choose to believe; if we believe in God's Word at all, we must choose to trust in all of it. The reality is that, because I accepted Christ, my transgressions had been separated from me as far as the East is from the West. That is the unfathomable grace of the gospel.

The more I chose to receive the gospel in my life, the more convicted I became to dedicate my life to him. I couldn't run away and hide anymore. I knew that I wouldn't be happy until I finally stopped and surrendered fully to him. I knew I needed to be right in my heart before I approached the throne of God for such a precious request as Haley's healing. I couldn't afford a break in my relationship with God; I didn't want anything, even a pang of unforgiveness or bitterness to stand between us.

I filled my life with his Word. On my way to work, which was one hour each way, I listened to tapes and used my time to praise and worship the Lord. I postured my spirit to bow down before his throne. At times, it was a very hard decision to worship instead of satisfying my flesh, but how good it felt to be freed from sin. It wasn't long before I was praying Psalm 23 regularly: hallowed be thy name...thy will be done. There's a lot of space between those two phrases, but once I fully embraced the grace of the gospel in my life, it became easier to give God the credit for everything I had and to praise him for everything he had done for me. It wasn't long before that love needed a place to go. Soon, it began to overflow out of me into others.

*****

One day, I was watching *The 700 Club* and witnessed how the "flying hospital" went around the world helping precious little children with horrible diseases and serious abnormalities. They seemingly had no money, no hope, and no future. I cried when I watched the images on the screen. Despite our challenges, Haley and I had everything we needed; these children didn't even have good food or clean water. I asked God to forgive me for being so selfish and thinking only of myself and my circumstances.

To reject my own victimhood, I decided to pledge a certain amount of money (even though I truly didn't have it) to benefit the flying hospital. It was a crazy act of faith, but I trusted God to provide. He did! I got so excited that I turned around and did it again. Ironically, the stress I had always carried from uncertain finances began to wane. One day, I was down to my last $100 and needed money to pay the nanny. Soon after, I got a call from a couple who felt led to help me with $200 a month! This money helped me pay the nanny. I thanked God for blessing me with a giving spirit and for providing for me in unexpected ways.

From that point on, I learned to set giving goals to contribute financially to different ministries. Being able to help those less fortunate than my family was a huge turning point for our family that opened up a lesson in love. More than loving Haley as my daughter, I started to love her for who she was as an individual. I started enjoying her instead of resenting her disabilities. I fell in love with her, and I know she could sense the change. She started to relax more. I would miss her so much when I would be at work. So many times I would get home too late to spend time with her. I would rush out the door in the morning and miss her again. The time I did have with her, I would cherish. She knew her mama loved her.

My love started to spill over to other people. I prayed on the way to work one day that God would give me a genuine love for everyone I came in contact with that day. Wow! What a difference it made in my attitude. I began to look at my clients differently and had an overwhelming desire to help them. That year, for the first time in thirteen years of land sales, I was ranked number one for sales and volume in our company! Financial success had never been my goal, but when I made loving people my ultimate goal, the benefits trickled into every area of my life.

CHAPTER 7

Wally

As I began to love people more, a new person emerged in my life. And from the very first time I met him, I felt that he would be the man I would marry. The company I worked for had a booth for land sales at the Houston Livestock Show and Rodeo. I dressed in my western duds and went down to the booth to work my shift. Next to me was a booth for all kinds of trucks accessories led by a handsome, charming divorcee. We began to chat and realized we had a lot in common. I told him I wanted to bring Haley, who was four at the time, to visit the Rodeo petting zoo later that week. In part, I wanted to see him again! While we stopped by to visit him later that week, he asked me out to dinner.

That date started a four-year courtship. One drawback of our relationship was that he lived an hour away from me. Even if we would only have fifteen minutes of quality time together because of Haley's care routine (feeding, bathing, and bedtime took longer than most children), the one-hour drive was still worth it to him. I was impressed by his patience with it all.

There was only one thing about Wally that bothered me, and that was he would hold Haley further out on his knees instead of close to his chest. He was great with kids, but it was clear he wasn't fully comfortable with her. I came to a decision that if I was going to entertain marriage, he would need to love Haley like I did.

I prayed all week. Finally, I decided to "throw a fleece." I told God that if Wally didn't feel a close connection with Haley by a certain date, it wouldn't be fair to us (or for him) to continue our relationship. We had a date scheduled on the Friday night I had in mind, and at that point I was still questioning his sentiments for Haley. While we were in the middle of dinner, I was formulating in my mind how I would break the news that our relationship couldn't continue under current circumstances. Not knowing this, and out of nowhere, he blurted out, "I don't know what happened, but I just love Haley!" I could tell by the tone of his voice that he was sincere. I knew that God had touched his heart at just the right time! That, and my parents blessing, was all I needed to accept his proposal.

Along with Wally, two other people came into my life: my stepsons, Nicolas and Grant. Only God could have known that when I considered baby names during the pregnancy, I had decided that I would name a girl "Haley Elizabeth" (Mom's middle name) and a boy "Grant Owen" (Dad's middle name). After Haley, I miraculously got my Grant also. Only God!

Wally and I were married in a small church ceremony on June 2, 2002. Haley was our flower girl!

Family picture of wedding

Marcia & Haley

Over time, we had issues with reliable caregivers, so we made a difficult decision for one of us to quit work. We jointly decided on a reversal of the traditional household roles, so Wally became "Mr. Mom." He handled the transition with flying colors! He spoiled me then and still does! He took over the laundry, cleaning, ironing, and continued to keep the cars spotless and the lawn mowed. He'd make food for the whole family, including special meals for Haley, and learned to bake a mean lemon cake. He said God told him before we were married to *be my strength*, and he certainly was.

Over time, Wally's love for Haley became apparent in every area possible. The school district relocated the special-needs education program to a different building that was far away with much earlier hours. Haley didn't adjust well to those early hours (taking after her mom!), so Wally began taking her to school every day in his truck. She loved that! When he got a four-wheeler, he made sure to take

Haley for rides on the nature trails by our house, even cross the shallow creek. She became a full-fledged daddy's girl!

When summer vacation came around, Wally told me that he was going to take Haley to Iowa to visit her grandparents for a couple of weeks.

"Really, just you two?" I responded

"Yep!" he replied enthusiastically.

Before I knew it, they went off on a two-day drive to Iowa. My brother Bill and his wife were halfway to the destination, so that was perfect for the first night's stop. The real challenge was finding places to heat up her food at mealtimes and places for diaper changes along the route. For feedings, he found the perfect solution by stopping at motels to use their microwave and table space. Everyone was very obliging. My parents were in heaven too! It gave them all great memories and created even more of a bond between father and daughter. Wally even found out she loved to jam to loud fifties music! It wasn't the last time they made that trip. How many fathers would do that? Surely, Wally had truly fallen in love with our daughter.

CHAPTER 8

An Attack

The enemy tries to rob, steal, and destroy in all areas of our lives: physical, spiritual, emotional, and mental. Throughout my life, I have sensed he has worked overtime to discourage me in my faith, but God has worked all things out for my good, so my determination is great. There was one week of my life in particular when the enemy used all his tactics to try to destroy the good things in our family's life.

Wally and I decided to take his boys (at that time, ages fourteen and seventeen) on a family vacation. It would be the first family vacation, and we were determined to go before they got jobs and became too busy for family time. We hired a woman from the neighborhood to take care of Haley for the week. She had babysat for her before and had a four-year-old of her own, so we thought that would be fun for Haley. We were so happy to have her helping us and felt secure in our decision. We left Monday morning and planned to return Saturday evening.

Wally and I missed Haley so much during the week and would often say we wished she could be with us. We knew, however, that the extra costs for her and a nanny to accompany us would have made the trip unaffordable. We called frequently throughout the week, at which point the caregiver would tell us she would smile at the sound of our voice. I had an uneasiness about leaving her, but everything seemed fine, so I dismissed my reservations as guilt.

On Saturday, we could hardly wait to hug and kiss our baby girl. We arrived home, and I bolted for the door. I ran into the family room to scoop her up but was mortified to find a frail, tiny frame of a child with dark eyes and an unresponsive glare. I could tell she was trying to smile. I picked her up, and she felt as light as a feather. I hurried her to Wally, who was equally horrified. I confronted the sitter then and demanded to know what Haley had eaten. She said she had eaten a good breakfast and opened the freezer door to show us what she had consumed. I was shocked to find the freezer shelf was still full of food, which should have been eaten throughout the week! She should have eaten at least nine jars of food per day; instead, she had only eaten about seven for the entire week! I was sick to my stomach when I realized the gravity what had happened. Wally was so upset he had to walk out while I told the sitter to call her ride.

Haley was unresponsive to our voices, so we rushed her out the door to the closest emergency room. Haley weighed in at twenty-four and a half pounds at eight years old! She had lost more than 25 percent of her body weight. After blood tests, the doctor told us that it was the worst case of dehydration he had seen in years. They ordered an ambulance and off we went to Texas Children's Hospital. We were there for a week until her sodium levels came up. Her pediatrician said it was a miracle she was alive, and another doctor said that after one more day without proper care she would not have survived. It took Haley at least three weeks to return back to her normal self. I truly believe Haley's angels were working overtime. It became clear to us that God had plans for her that Satan can't destroy.

"No one can snatch them out of my Father's hand" (John 20:28).

*****

One day, our nine-year-old neighbor, Pryscylla, came over to visit Haley. She wanted to learn to feed Haley, she said, so she could earn a little money on the weekends. I thought it was good for Haley to hear the voices of children her own age, so I agreed. None of the neighborhood kids came to play because she couldn't respond. You

43

can't blame them. Even in school the kids don't talk. It had to be boring for her. I would follow people with kids around in the grocery store and Wal-Mart just so she could hear the children. Wally would take her to the mall and ride on the merry-go-round bench too. She would get excited and seemed more *talkative* when she got home. Pryscylla and I were talking at the kitchen table one day when I told her the word the Pastor had said to us a few weeks prior. In response, she replied, "Our Sunday school teacher told us that if we *hoped* for something that someday it *might happen*, but if we *prayed* for something it would *happen*." Then she told me about a dream she had about Haley. It was even in color. She said she saw Haley healed and that they were having a tea party. Out of the mouth of babes! God said in Matthew 38:2–4 "to come as a little child" with childlike faith, in other words. They don't question or come with excess baggage. That's the kind of faith he wants from us. Haley was healed, so her friend wanted to party with her!

Do dreams come true? Maybe they're a form of confirmation depending on the timing and circumstance. Pryscylla's dream had both for me, and I clung to it. I started visualizing Haley playing tea party with Pryscylla the way my mom and I did when I was little, and I felt the mood in the room. I envisioned the celebration and excitement as Haley experienced her first birthday as the perfect child God had created to be born. I watched her expressions, heard the fluctuation in her voice, and enjoyed her vivid imagination. She was so carefree that no one would suspect that she had been bound inside herself just weeks before. A total, complete miracle by the human standard just seems too hard to imagine. It was exciting, to say the least, to think about the actual day of her healing.

Think of the most important dinner party you have ever planned or maybe a big surprise party. The hours of preparation, the time invested, and certainly the energy and thoughts involved with pulling off such a successful event were worthwhile.

It occurred to me that I didn't have a plan after God healed Haley! My mind had carried me to that point as the end. I had so much emotion wrapped up in the end goal that I had neglected to plan the party!

Who would I tell first and how? Oh my gosh, this is going to be fun! It's like planning an exciting vacation. The anticipation, I think, is as much fun as the trip. Your spirits are high, daily routines and little annoyances somehow don't have the same negative effect. It's like, let it happen, I don't care, I'm going to be out of here for a whole week in a few days! So I started planning that first day.

First, I would call my mom and dad and say, "Grandma and Grandpa, get on different phones there is someone here that would like to talk to you!" "Hi, Grandma and Grandpa, it's Haley! God healed me! I love you" she would say in her sweet little voice. I'm sure there would be dead silence and then bursts of emotions ranging from joy to tears of joy! Next will be similar phone calls to Uncle Bill and Aunt Monetta, and Aunt Donna. Grandma and Grandpa in Louisiana are on that list and her birth dad.

Now, there are those I would not want to call but would want to have the fun of *presenting* her in person. My brother and his wife that live up the street top that list. If it is a workday, we would drive to Houston to where my brother works and announce that Uncle Steve has a visitor! I can picture him coming around the corner, seeing her and running to her with a face full of tears and full embraces! I'm sure he will take the rest of the day off, if possible.

Now, on to Aunt Elaine's place of employment. Haley will arrive with a beautiful bouquet of flowers that she got to pick out herself. Since she never could see well, she was just in awe and wonder with their beauty. Aunt Elaine would shed no less tears than Uncle Steve had. We would have both places and coworkers in utter chaos!

My coworkers aren't all on shifts together, but we will make that emotional visit and calls.

If school is in session, we will make a grand appearance to all of her teachers she had in the last six years at her special-needs school.

We have to go on a neighborhood walk, proclaiming the good news of Jesus's healing preparing her for her future ministry. I can't wait for her to see Pryscylla, her little friend from across the street. Now they can play tea party! So many people to call and share with that have been a big part of her life and some of her nannies, Ms. Betty in Trinidad, Amanda, and Ms. Flora, or Granny, we used to call her, is celebrating in heaven. Our church family that has been such a strong emotional support heard about it. News traveled fast before we even made it to church on Sunday. Aunt Elaine will be busy on the Internet sharing pictures with cousins from coast to coast. The president of the company I work for requires a personal visit so he can see my *faith goal* has been completed! I imagine our house will be in turmoil for quite a while with visits. It won't take my mom and dad long to pack a suitcase, and I see a shopping trip in our near future!

I wrote a letter to the Osteens at Lakewood Church telling them that Haley was there for prayer at about six months old and how Dodie had prayed over her and had given me healing scriptures to read to her at night. I received a call back asking if I might share with the congregation on a Sunday morning. I had a vision of speaking at Lakewood Church driving home from work one time. I was nervous but anxiously agreed. We went over what I might share and we met them before the service for prayer.

What an exciting and powerful experience. I was afraid I might start to cry as I was talking, and I couldn't let thousands of people nationwide see my mascara run down my face, so just in case I would wear waterproof mascara that day! I called relatives to let them know Haley and I would be on TV and to watch. As I was introduced, I prayed silently for calmness and that I wouldn't trip going up the stairs. I looked around at all the people in that great auditorium and started to speak. The Holy Spirit took over from there, and I didn't even remember afterward what I said. As I introduced Haley and she walked up the stage to meet me, she was greeted with a standing ovation and applause that seemed to go on forever. As the applause died down, she thanked everyone that might be watching who had prayed for her and that her favorite thing was to ride her bicycle and tea parties! We gave God all the glory, in Jesus's name, then the tears began to flow! Thank God for that waterproof mascara!

We were given the privilege of praying with people, the people who came forward for prayer who needed healing in that special segment of the service along with the Osteens and others from the church. After the two services I was tired, but on such a high it took us a few days to get back to normal, whatever that was.

Haley and I had watched TBN and CBN for several years. I would burn up the 800 number at times for prayer from whomever answered the prayer line at *The 700 Club*. Helping Operation Blessing kept my mind off of our needs and onto others. It was a big part of my sanity. "It's more blessed to give than to receive" (Acts 20:35). I had to let Pat and Terri know to thank them for the part they had played in our lives.

We received an exciting call asking if we would be open to do a short segment with Terri on the show! What an exciting experience, and off we went to Virginia Beach on Haley's first plane ride with no handicaps. It was our prayer that God would touch people in their living rooms. Within a short time of the airing, we had tons of mail! I heard from friends I had lost contact with years ago. We received touching letters to pray for others in great physical need and parents of special needs children wanting prayer and encouragement. It took a long time to follow up with the mail, but not one went unanswered. A few of them received phone calls and a promise to keep in touch, which I still do today. The Lord had started to open doors for the calling on our lives and Haley's prophecy to be fulfilled for precious souls to come to Jesus. It was all worth it!

The food tasting was fun. It was a whole new world, trying out all sorts of solid foods to determine what she did and did not like. She did discover chocolate! She is truly her mother's daughter.

I used to wonder when she was healed how we would catch her up on her school level, but God took care of that too. I guess he had her taking classes in her sleep at night.

I have been excitedly writing about my daughter's future healing, and I was hit with an overwhelming sense of loss. It was so real I don't even know how to write my feelings right now. And you're thinking, "How could you feel a loss being absorbed in her healing?" God wanted me to be prepared for something that I hadn't even thought about, and that is that I lost my *baby*. She was still there, but she was totally a different person. She went from being totally dependent on my husband and I for everything to being replaced by an independent mind of her own, young lady. I had been still rocking her at night. She was small for her age, and even though there were feelings of pure joy, I went through a horrific sense of loss. Does that make any sense? I went through a low time, a bit of depression, preparing to let go. Other parents see a slow transition as their kids grow and age. I guess it's a little how parents feel when their kids go off to college. I didn't want any of those feelings to overshadow the gratitude and joy to God. I thank God for preparing me ahead of time and for planting that thought even before she was healed so I could deal with it early. Can you imagine a God who is so in tune to our innermost being and so intimate to our needs? Wow! I did know that if he cares for me that much to let me know ahead of time that I would experience a downside in the midst of a joyful experience that he too would help me through.

This day feels different to me. I have a peace, a joy that passes all understanding. I feel like a bright light shines all around me enveloping me with a warmth and love direct from heaven. Last night I went to sleep with anticipation. I awoke with a start. Am I dreaming? I don't think so. I do hear my daughter crying. It wasn't like any other night. Yes, she is crying "Mama, Mama!" I wanted to spring from my bed, but I woke Wally up first and we both sprung from the bed. Tears were already rolling down our cheeks. The few seconds to reach her door seemed like an eternity. I cried, "Mommy's here, Haley." As Wally turned on the light, we saw her sitting up in bed for the first time in her life. I scooped her up. I didn't want to scare her. We both hugged her and cried and reassured her. A sweet presence filled her room, I can't even describe. My heart, my mind, and my emotions are flooded with these thoughts. This is how I expected our miracle to happen, however, God had other plans.

CHAPTER 9

To Playground

January 26, 2007, was a day like any other day, except I had gotten a late start and was rushing to get ready for work. Haley was still in bed, and I decided not to wake her up to kiss her goodbye. I rushed off to work and, when I arrived, two of my coworkers were already there. I usually started my work day reading the paper, usually focusing on the "Funnies" section so I could begin my day with a laugh. I heard the phone rang, and my colleague Kelly answered it.

I wasn't paying much attention, but my ears perked up when I heard him ask, "Wally?" I knew he was talking about my manager when I heard him say, "She's not here." I wondered why he would want to talk to my manager and why he wasn't asking to talk to me. Kelly called over another coworker and murmured something to her in a low voice. She walked away momentarily and then walked in my direction. She turned away, her back to me, and then attempted in my direction again. She didn't say a word and finally started pacing.

"Penny, are you okay?" I asked her.

Finally, she came over to me, and I stood up to meet her. She looked into my face and said, "Marcia, sit down." The pained look on her face said it all; she didn't have to say a word. Horror washed over me.

I remember a blood-curdling scream coming out of my mouth. I remember jumping up and running out of the room. I screamed

"No, no, no" repeatedly, and finally, "I hate you, God!" I left everything and ran out to my car.

Penny followed me outside and drove me home. When we arrived, I flew in the door and ran upstairs to Haley's room. There was Haley, wrapped in Wally's loving arms while he rocked her in her rocking chair. He slowly stood up and lovingly handed our precious little girl to me.

The events that followed were a blur. I knew that people were in my house, but I didn't know who they were. Time made no sense to me, and I held on to Haley as they came in and out. At various points, my family and coworkers came to visit. The pastor of our church came to pray for us. I still believed that a miracle was possible and implored him to please pray for Haley's resurrection. As I held her, he prayed, but nothing happened. I know he just did that for me. Then he told me something I will never forget.

He said that on his drive to our home, he had a vision of Haley running in a field in heaven. While she was running, she had fallen down. In the vision, Jesus walked over to Haley. He couldn't see Jesus's face; the only part of Jesus that was visible was his hand reaching down to help her up.

"There was one thing about Jesus's hand that puzzled me," the pastor admitted as he looked into my eyes. He explained that when Jesus reached his hand down to Haley, he was almost making a fist; four of his fingers were closed and his thumb was sticking out. He thought it odd but felt that it was an important part of the vision to share.

I was stunned. I explained to him that, because of her condition, Haley's hands were always tight. She couldn't open her fingers freely. She could only open her hand enough for her to grab your thumb. There was no way that the pastor could have known that detail, and somehow it brought confirmation that Haley was indeed with Jesus. Even so, knowing she was with him somehow didn't ease my pain.

Other people arrived. I saw a policeman in the hallway and another man who I guessed was the coroner. I couldn't bear to let them take my baby away, but so much time had elapsed that they really needed to take her. In a flood of tears, Wally and I chose clothes for and dressed our baby girl before she was taken downstairs to a gurney. Wally and I, along with my brother and sister-in-law, said our painful goodbyes and stayed behind.

As I walked through the house, there were other people present, but I couldn't tell you who they were. I noticed my work family had already brought food for us. I began reaching out to Haley's birth father, her grandparents, and teachers. Word got around quickly, so many at the school already knew.

After I said goodbye to Haley, I pretty much stayed in bed. Wally and I were exhausted from the grief; we would sleep for a very short time and wake up sobbing. We knew we needed to make funeral and burial arrangements but couldn't wrap our minds around that yet. The next day, when a sweet neighbor asked us what cemetery we were choosing, we admitted we had no idea. She made a recommendation, and it worked out perfectly. A colleague, with more experience in the funeral industry than we had, led us through the preparation process and helped us make wise decisions.

When someone is grieving because of a death, I found out what *not* to say. One thing was, "Well, she's with Jesus, she's happy now, or she's better off." I wanted her here with me! I'm selfish. I would have done anything to get her back. At that time, it wasn't comforting for me to hear that. I know people feel they need to say something. "I'm so sorry" is fine and a long hug.

In 1 John 1:1–44 it tells the story of Lazarus's death. His sister came to Jesus and told him his dear friend had died. Jesus was in another town. He could have spoken a word from where he was and Lazarus could have come back to life, but he didn't. He showed us how to be a friend instead. He went to the city and home of Lazarus and cried with their family. He felt their pain. He was already buried. He knew he was going to raise Lazarus, but he showed them true compassion first, then he raised him!

I learned a lesson on how to be a true friend from a lot of our friends and neighbors. The second night after Haley died, while I was in bed crying, our neighbor, Krystyna, walked into the bedroom, put on a tape of soothing music, and she stroked my forehead until I fell asleep.

We chose a beautiful dress for Haley's burial; it was the same one she wore to her first and only prom. A good friend went out to find the perfect color of pink nail polish for her. I still felt so protective over Haley; I really didn't want anyone at the funeral home to touch her. So together with my sister-in-law and a few close friends, we went to the funeral home to paint Haley's nails and curl her hair. A precious friend, Shirley, brought a small, silver heart-shaped box so I could save a lock of her hair.

There were so many other decisions to make. When we purchased Haley's grave plot, we decided to purchase plots on each side of her for Wally and I. We started looking for a grave marker for the head of her cemetery plot; it all seemed so final. When we saw a *Pooh Bear* stone, we both knew that was the one for our girl, whom we had always called *Haley Bear*. It had two honeypots on each side for flowers. A friend helped us write an obituary and pick out a picture for the paper.

In the midst of having to make decisions, people rallied around us. Haley's Uncle Bill sang in a gospel quartet and had recorded "Welcome to Heaven, My Child" and "Jesus Loves Me." We decided to play both during the service. Another coworker asked me to go through pictures and offered to have a photo slideshow set to music documenting Haley's life. Karen and Penny offered to fly out-of-state guests who didn't have the funds to come to the funeral, which meant my Aunt Maxine and Uncle George from Minnesota and our precious Betty from Trinidad were able to come to town. Someone set up a memorial fund, and many people gave to it. The tangible love of those around us was absolutely overwhelming. We can never repay them for all they did.

The night before the funeral, we hosted a visitation. For two hours, we received a steady stream of caring people. Haley's teachers and classmates were among those who came to say goodbye. At one point in the evening, I glanced up to see David, one of Haley's favorite classmates, being pushed down the aisle in his wheelchair by his mother. I let out a cry and burst into tears. Haley and David had ridden the same school bus together for a number of years, and even though neither of them could speak, it was evident they shared a bond. His mom explained that when she told David about Haley's death that he understood and had grieved at the news.

The husband of a coworker told me when he was at visitation, that he also had a vision of Haley in heaven. Apparently, she had learned to skip! He said, "She's a skipper!" I wanted so badly to have a vision of her too.

The next day, the funeral home was full. So many people had come to see Haley. Her relatives from Louisiana, including her birth father and his family, came to pay their respects. Special friends I hadn't seen for a long time came. The owner of the company I worked for closed the office so all their employees could come. My former boss and the sales crew from my previous land project came. The list went on, our hearts touched by their presence.

I grieve that my own family was not fully represented at Haley's funeral. I was still mourning the loss of my father, who had passed away four months prior. I desperately needed my mom, but she was unable to attend the funeral, as she had slipped into dementia, at least in part, because she was still in shock and grief over my dad's death. My older brother, Bill, who had been one of Haley's nannies during a season when I needed backup childcare, had to stay in Iowa to care for my mother and wasn't able to attend the funeral. It was hard to deal with all the loss. Gratefully, other family members and friends surrounded us with love. My aunt and uncle, who stood in as my parents, and thirty plus flower arrangements lining the chapel reminded us of how many old and new friends were supporting us that day. We could literally feel love radiating from each one of those arrangements as we read the names and condolences.

Right before the service was to start, the attendant came up and told us as we were sitting in the front row and everyone was seated that the music tape that had been done for us wouldn't work. That meant my Brother Bill's songs wouldn't be a part of it. That brought tears. She suggested a Celine Dion song "My Heart will Go On." I wasn't familiar with it, but Elaine, my sister-in-law, said it would be good.

The night before the funeral, God had given me the idea to make a bouquet using a flower or leaf from each arrangement to place beside Haley.

During that song, Wally and I started at opposite sides of the chapel, where we pulled a flower or leaf from each of her arrangements. The song ended perfectly as we met at the casket. We tied the bouquet together with a piece of lace she had worn to her first and only prom and laid it next to her. We took our seat in the front row, as a video played showing photos of Haley's life, I went numb.

After the video, Amanda, the young high school girl who was her summer nanny for two years, spoke and so did her mom, Kathy. It was so sweet. Donna from work wrote a heart-wrenching memorial. It is printed at the end of this book.

Determined that we wanted to showcase the glory of God during Haley's funeral, I asked the pastor to present an invitation for attendees to accept the Lord at the end of the service. He worked it in beautifully. At the invitation, seven people raised their hand and accepted Christ that day. With the two who had already accepted the Lord while in our house, Haley helped usher nine people into a relationship with God. Praise God!

*****

In the months after Haley's death, a beautiful park was built in the neighborhood where I was selling land for custom homes. To commemorate Haley's life, the owner of my company, Tom and his wife, donated a special-needs saddle. My boss's son, Eric, and his wife made sure the park had swings for children with special needs. Today, children in wheelchairs can wheel up the platform and swing back and forth. The first person to use it was Haley's special friend, David!

My mind saw Haley playing on *our* playground, but the two people who had seen Haley on heaven's playground after she died, cemented in my mind the title of this book.

CHAPTER 10

The Healing Process

But those who wait on the Lord shall renew their strength;
they shall mount up with wings like eagles, they shall
run and not be weary, they shall walk and not faint.

—Isaiah 40:31

In the days and weeks after Haley's death, I experienced a roller coaster of emotions. One of them was anger. In faith, I had always believed that Haley would be healed from all sickness and disease; I had focused on this faith goal for eleven years. I have believed that, one day, I would write a book about her healing and had already titled it *From Wheelchair to Playground*. When Haley passed away, I directed my anger at God. I was mad at him for not healing Haley and for letting her die. I felt as though he had abandoned us. I still spoke to him and I still loved him, but there were times when I just couldn't deal with him!

What do you do when you feel abandoned by God? Even the godliest of men and women have felt, at least one time in their lives, abandoned by God. If you haven't had a traumatic experience, you most likely will in your lifetime. I felt that total abandonment when I lost my daughter, my only child. We conjure up so many reasons why He must have left us high and dry, or taken a loved one from us. We take it personally: that loss, that health issue, that job we were sure we would get. Now, we're disillusioned, alone. We used to feel the Holy Spirit all over us but not anymore.

Who moved? Where did he go? Jesus was God but also human, just like us. He felt all the feelings that we have ever felt. You may revel in this lonely separation for a time but realize that you don't want to be there forever. You can ask yourself, "Do I want to fight my way back or stay in this feeling of separation?" Hebrews 13:5 says, "For He Himself has said, 'I will never leave you or forsake you.'" If we are honest with ourselves, we know in our hearts we're the ones that moved, not God. We read our Bibles more in those times.

My life in church and reading my Bible led me to a faith that God answers your prayers, and I had that faith. I felt I had mustard-seed faith to tell that mountain to move, and God even gave me that faith. I claimed scripture after scripture. Where did I miss it? Was there more that I overlooked somewhere? Where did I fail that didn't give Haley the full life she deserved? I know she would have been good in sports. I could *see* her running marathons and me in the stands cheering. My dreams were just a pile of ash now. What do I have to look forward to? I can't even go there in my mind yet. I feel dead inside, with no hope and no future. I just needed to get through the funeral. I had to get back to work. I didn't feel like it, but I knew it would at least keep my mind off of things and it was time.

Eventually, the anger turned to numbness. I felt dead inside, as though I had no hope and nothing to look forward to. When it was time to return to work, I felt like I couldn't even complete a full sentence. My mind just wouldn't engage. I felt I couldn't sell coal to an Eskimo. Even in my dismissal of him, God began to breathe life back into me. In my place of work, he began to talk through me and just took over for me. Sales fell into my lap with no effort, sometimes two and three land purchases at a time. My performance was so obviously out of the ordinary that even my coworkers mentioned God's exceptional favor on me.

My anger toward God turned to guilt when I began to recognize all he was doing for me. I was number one in sales that year, and God continued showering us with favor. Despite our extra expenses, we had never stopped tithing. More than that, we finally got to save for the future. His love never fails.

Despite God's great love for me, guilt tore me apart inside. Out of everything I experienced, it was my most prevalent and nagging emotion. Even as time went on, I continuously revisited memories from the past. Haley's arms and legs were very skinny. Kids in wheelchairs don't have muscle that adds to a person's weight, so it's normal that they weigh less for their age. I fed her balanced meals so she wasn't fat, which wouldn't be good for her. For some reason she started not eating much. It was time to see a doctor for mobility, etc., and I was led somehow to a new doctor. He told me she was too small and she should be on a feeding tube so she could develop properly. He made me feel so guilty. I immediately scheduled an appointment at TCH to see a doctor regarding a feeding tube. She enjoyed eating though and loved her pumpkin pie filling for dessert. But for some reason, he made me feel like a horrible mother. I scheduled a time for the feeding tube surgery. Her regular doctor was unable to come and she had been already prepped for surgery, so I agreed to let another doctor operate on her.

When I saw her after surgery, the tube sticking out of her stomach was huge, not at all like the others I had seen. Even the nurses were surprised by its size. I found out later that the doctor had found an old tube on a shelf and used it. It never fit right, and the wound didn't heal properly.

After that surgery, Haley never smiled again. The feeding tube became a constant challenge, and we frequently had to take Haley to the emergency room because the liquid food we gave her would leak around the tube. I was so upset by the surgery results and blamed myself for allowing a different doctor to conduct the surgery and for even agreeing to a feeding tube at all! We scheduled a date for corrective surgery on Monday, but Haley passed away on the previous Friday. I blamed myself for her death, because I felt she was so miserable, she just gave up.

Guilt compelled me to pull away from people, busy myself in activities, and hide from relationships. Wally and I fought more and distance grew between us. Shopping became a literal escape to retreat from the memories and tension our house bore. I shopped after work and on my days off. I wasn't dwelling in the shelter of the Most High God; I was dwelling in the shelter of the shopping mall. Shopping became a temporary gratification but never helped me deal with my grief. I replaced the healing power of God with a misguided idol. Idols can present themselves when we are seeking replacement therapy. I needed the healing that only God could provide, and it was a long time before I gave him the chance. What I found was, there is a thin line between our pursuit of happiness and idol worship.

Grief has a natural process, and we can choose to grieve with God or without him. For the first few years after Haley's death, I chose to grieve without him. As guilt gnawed at me, the enemy gained a foothold in my life. Ultimately, this made healing impossible.

When a few of my friends told me I needed to address my guilt before it killed me, I asked for God's help. This started by asking him to bring to mind people I needed to forgive. This was a slow process. I think it took me a long time to forgive myself because I had the mistaken notion that my grief kept Haley alive. I was afraid that if I gave up grieving that I would lose my precious memories of her. How the enemy will twist and deceive.

Not moving on from a loss will cause you other great losses. Those can be of friends, happiness, and abundant blessings from God for your future. No one wants to be around a bitter person, and sooner or later, you'll be left alone to wallow in it by yourself.

Recognize if you are feeling stuck on one negative emotion, or if others see it in you, listen to them. The choice of life or death is ours, and death can be an emotional death. Work through it. You may be in a state longer than someone else would be, but don't feel too proud to get help from a Christian counselor. I say Christian counselor because I've had experience with non-Christian ones and I don't want you to go there.

It's easy to trust when things are going well. God will keep skimming off the *dregs*. When metal gets very hot in a pot, the impurities float to the top. As we get through a difficult step, one at a time, God will skim the imperfections off of us and when we are done, we will reveal purity, a fine treasured image. I wasn't consumed and you won't be either.

Believe that only the Lord can handle anything you're going through, just don't give into it or give root to it again. Don't speak it over yourself.

We grow physically in stages in our lives and it is no different with our spiritual lives. It would be so cool to have all wisdom and knowledge from adolescence to adulthood, but it doesn't work that way. God took every hour, every day, every raw emotion to slowly, subtlety transform me in a lot of different areas, just a little tweak at a time. I probably would have rebelled if he'd hit me with full frontal force.

You will get there and, believe it or not, you will find joy again. There was a song we sang as kids to the tune of "Jingle Bells" in Bible school called "Joy." "Joy, joy, this is what it means/J, Jesus first/Y, yourself last/and O, others in between" and repeat. When you are stuck in one of the grieving processes, you are putting the Y in front. You are putting your emotions—the grief, the bitterness, the self-ishness, the anger, the disillusionment—out in front of Jesus and others. You will never experience *joy* again until you spell it right! Ask Jesus to heal all of those deep disappointments and bring them to the surface so you can deal with them. Satan wants you to hold onto them in the depths to hold you bondage and steal from you. Realize it's him and not you keeping you prisoner. Demand that he let your emotions go in the name of Jesus! Say it out loud!

When I allowed God to address my heart, he gently showed me that I had allowed my grief to keep me inwardly focused. In ignoring those around me, I had missed the fact that Wally was hurting too. I left him on his own to grieve, and he felt abandoned by me. Where I thought grief and guilt were keeping Haley alive, the consumption of guilt in my life was actually stealing the good memories I had of her. That could have ruined our marriage. I know a lot of parents will split after the loss of a child, because one will move on before the other. They may claim the *blame game* and people grieve in dif-ferent ways. Sometimes emotional grieving is kept inside or can be expressed as anger. Even though we clung to each other, I had pulled away without realizing it!

There came a day where God spoke, "Enough!" over my life. That night I had gone to a Sunday night service where anyone needing healing was invited to the altar. I'm sure the pastor was thinking, "Oh, not her again!" Still, I went forward for prayer. I didn't feel differently after the prayer, but when I returned to my seat I saw a picture in my mind of a heart torn into two pieces. I heard God say to me, "You don't love your husband as you should." In that moment, I began to recognize the way that I had allowed Haley's death to destroy my life. God reminded me that I was holding back my love for Wally because I was afraid to love someone who I could lose. In an instant, my desire to connect with him and love him returned in full force. Whereas it had previously felt impossible to love through my grief, it was suddenly as though my heart was fully and miraculously healed. I had never felt such joy! As I asked Wally for forgiveness, God began to heal my grief. I testified the experience in church that God replaced my sadness with joy and a renewed love for my husband. I not only had a love for my husband like I had never felt, but it overflowed to other people too.

*****

Since having Haley, my life will never be the same. Early on in her life, God gave me the unnatural faith to believe in Haley's healing. I don't know why He did that, but I do know that faith helped me survive many challenging days and nights throughout her life. Through her life and her death, he has used faith to draw me closer to him than I ever thought possible. As difficult as moments of my life have been, I can testify that leaning on his arms in times of sorrow and grief have revealed God's immense love for me in ways I never could have imagined before Haley was born. More than that, I have come to understand the sovereignty of God and embrace the reality that he, and he alone, is in control.

Like many parents have for their children, I had a vision for Haley's life: healing. I believed that, with public testimony and phenomenal fanfare, Haley would one day give glory to God for the miraculous physical transformation of her body. I had faith for a day when she would leap out of her wheelchair fully healed and play on the playground with other physically healthy children. Instead, Haley leapt out of the physical limitations of her earthly body and into heaven's playground. Having completed her earthly assignment, giving glory to God through the simple worship of her short life on earth, Haley now runs unrestrained by the bonds of sickness, disease, or time; she gives glory to God by playing in his presence for all eternity forward.

I would never have had it any other way.

EPILOGUE

You have shown me great and severe troubles, shall revive me again, and bring me up again from the depths of the earth. You shall increase my greatness and comfort me on every side.

—Psalms 71:20–21

Aunt Donna & Haley

Haley didn't like the snow

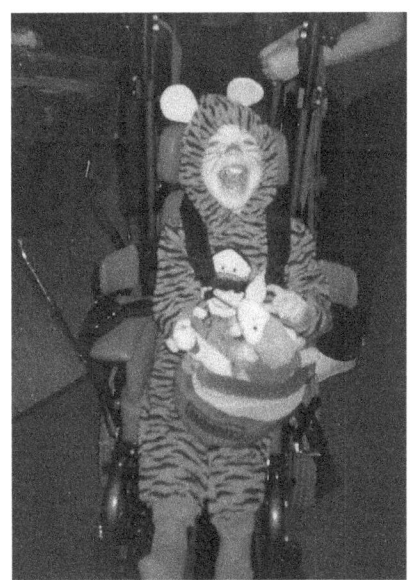

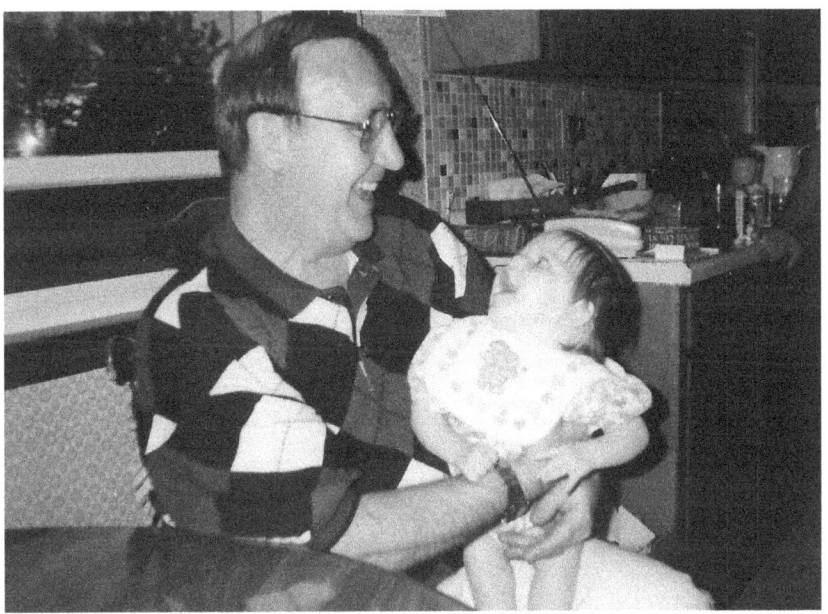

Uncle Bill & Haley

Uncle Steve and Haley.

Beginning of this book on post it notes

As Haley transitioned from her wheelchair to God's playground, marking the completion of her earthly assignment, I was left on earth to accomplish mine. Part of that assignment involves commemorating how—through the fullness of her joy and the brightness of her smile—Haley Elizabeth impacted the lives of those around her. Part of it involves continuing to serve others through the compassion God has given me in the years following her death. And part of it involves sharing the lessons I've learned about loss and grief through the penning of this book. I invite you consider them if you are currently navigating your way through grief.

Move Close to God

First, if you are experiencing grief, know that there's a natural order for grieving and allow yourself time to experience each step fully. Move through each one and don't allow yourself to be consumed by them. Even if it feels as though you're taking baby steps, move forward and move toward him. In moments when you move away from him, ask him for forgiveness. (1 John 1:9)

Tell God how You Feel

Next, tell God how you feel. Psalms 42:2 says, "I pour out my complaint before Him; I declare before Him my trouble." Do that. Unload your cares on him. He used every hour and every raw emotion I surrendered to him to subtly transform me from the inside out. He wants to do the same with you.

Ask God to Heal Your Heart

Psalms 147:3, "He heals the brokenhearted and binds up their wounds." Oh, how I have claimed that verse! Malachi 4:2, "But to you who fear My name, the sun of righteousness shall arise with healing in His wings, and you shall go out and grow fat like stall fed calves." Another version says, "You shall be like leaping calves from the stall." If we ask, the Light of the world will arise and settle all around us with total and complete healing. Ask for God's healing. He's waiting to bless you in unimaginable ways.

Praise God in All Things

During my healing process, I visited Psalm 103:1–5 often, "Bless the Lord O my soul; And all that is within me, bless His holy name! Bless the Lord, O my soul, and forget not all His benefits; Who forgives all your iniquities, who heals all your diseases. Who redeems your life from destruction, who crowns you with loving kindness and tender mercies, Who satisfies your mouth with good things, so that your youth is renewed like the eagle's." If we don't seek emotional healing after loss, we will lose greatly in other ways. Praise God in the healing process, hard as it may seem.

Hold onto Hope

When you watch your child experience difficulty or pain, hope is what keeps you alive. As I look back at Haley's life, I'm grateful God didn't tell me what he knew was going to happen. My hope for Haley's healing kept me fully engaged in her life and prevented me from giving up on our life. I encourage you to pray and meditate on Scripture and not to lose hope. You only have one life, and God doesn't want you to spend it in the depths of despair; he wants you to have life and live it to the fullest! If you surrender yourself to him, emotions and all, you will be amazed at where he'll take you!

> Blessed be the God and Father of our Lord Jesus Christ the Father of mercies and God of all comfort, who comforts us in all our tribulation that we may be able to comfort those who are in trouble with the comfort with which we ourselves are comforted by God. (2 Corinthians 1:3–4)

> The grass withers and flowers fade, but the word of God shall stand forever. (Isaiah 40:8)

A NOTE TO THE READER

Dear Reader,

If you are praying for healing, I encourage you to meditate on and pray these scriptures daily. Trust them and believe them; thank God for them and wait for his timing! Everyone's outcome may be different.

I love you, and so does God!

—Marcia

Healing Scriptures (New Living Translation)

If you will listen carefully to the voice of the Lord your God and do what is right in his sight, obeying his commands and laws, then I will not make you suffer the diseases I sent on the Egyptians; for I am the Lord who heals you. (Exodus 15:26)

You must serve only the Lord your God. If you do, I will bless you with food and water, and I will keep you healthy. (Exodus 23:25)

And the Lord will protect you from all sickness. He will not let you suffer from the terrible diseases you knew in Egypt, but he will bring them all on your enemies! (Deuteronomy 7:15)

Today I have given you the choice between life and death, between blessings and curses. I call on heaven and earth to witness the choice you make. Oh, that you would choose life, that you and your descendants might live! 20 Choose to love the Lord your God and to obey him and commit yourself to him, for he is your life. Then you will live long in the land the Lord swore to give your ancestors Abraham, Isaac, and Jacob. (Deuteronomy 30:19–20)

Praise the Lord, I tell myself; with my whole heart, I will praise his holy name. Praise the Lord, I tell myself, and never forget the good things he does for me. He forgives all my sins and heals all my diseases. He ransoms me from death and surrounds me with love and tender mercies. He fills my life with good things. My youth is renewed like the eagle's! The Lord gives righteousness and justice to all who are treated unfairly. He revealed his character to Moses and his deeds to the people of Israel. The Lord is merciful and gracious; he is slow to get angry and full of unfailing love. He will not constantly accuse us, nor remain angry forever. He has not punished us for all our sins, nor does he deal with us as we deserve. For his unfailing love toward those who fear him is as great as the height of the heavens above the earth. (Psalm 103:1–11)

He spoke, and they were healed—snatched from the door of death. (Psalm 107:20)

I will not die, but I will live to tell what the Lord has done. (Psalm 118:17)

Pay attention, my child, to what I say. Listen carefully. Don't lose sight of my words. Let them penetrate deep within your heart, for they bring life and radiant health to anyone who discovers their meaning. Above all else, guard your heart, for it affects everything you do. (Proverbs 4:20–23)

Don't be afraid, for I am with you. Do not be dismayed, for I am your God. I will strengthen you. I will help you. I will uphold you with my victorious right hand. (Isaiah 41:10)

Yet it was our weaknesses he carried; it was our sorrows that weighed him down. And we thought his troubles were a punishment from God for his own sins! But he was wounded and crushed for our sins. He was beaten that we might have peace. He was whipped, and we were healed! (Isaiah 53:4–5)

"Will give you back your health and heal your wounds," says the Lord. (Jeremiah 30:17)

Suddenly, a man with leprosy approached Jesus. He knelt before him, worshiping, "Lord," the man said, "if you want to, you can make me well again." Jesus touched him. "I want to," he said. "Be healed!" And instantly the leprosy disappeared. This fulfilled the word of the Lord through Isaiah, who said, "He took our sicknesses and removed our diseases." (Matthew 8:2–3, 17)

I tell you this: Whatever you prohibit on earth is prohibited in heaven, and whatever you allow on earth is allowed in heaven. I also tell you this: If two of you agree down here on earth concerning anything you ask, my Father in heaven will do it for you. (Matthew 18:18–19)

When Jesus told them, "I assure you, if you have faith and don't doubt, you can do things like this and much more. You can even say to this mountain, 'May God lift you up and throw you into the sea,' and it will happen. If you believe, you will receive whatever you ask for in prayer." (Matthew 21:21–22)

I assure you that you can say to this mountain, "May God lift you up and throw you into the sea," and your command will be obeyed. All that's required is that you really believe and do not doubt in your heart. Listen to me! You can pray for anything, and if you believe you will have it." (Mark 11:23–24)These signs will accompany those who believe. They will cast out demons in my name, and they will speak new languages. They will be able to handle snakes with safety, and if they drink anything poisonous, it won't hurt them. They will be able to place their hands on the sick and heal them. (Mark 16:17–18)

The thief's purpose is to steal and kill and destroy. My purpose is to give life in all its fullness. (John 10:10)

That is what the Scriptures mean when God told him, "I have made you the father of many nations." This happened because Abraham believed in the God who brings the dead back to life and who brings into existence what didn't exist before. When God promised Abraham that he would become the father of many nations, Abraham believed him. God had also said, "Your descendants will be as numerous as the stars," even though such a promise seemed utterly impossible! And Abraham's faith did not weaken, even though he knew that he was too old to be a father at the age of one hundred and that Sarah, his wife, had never been able to have children. Abraham never wavered in believing God's promise. In fact, his faith grew stronger, and in this he brought glory to God. (Romans 4:17–20)

The Spirit of God, who raised Jesus from the dead, lives in you. And just as he raised Christ from the dead, he will give life to your mortal body by this same Spirit living within you. (Romans 8:11)

We use God's mighty weapons, not mere worldly weapons, to knock down the Devil's strongholds. With these weapons we break down every proud argument that keeps people from knowing God. With these weapons we conquer their rebellious ideas, and we teach them to obey Christ. (2 Corinthians 10:4–5)

But Christ has rescued us from the curse pronounced by the law. When he was hung on the cross, he took upon himself the curse for our wrongdoing. For it is written in the Scriptures, "Cursed is everyone who is hung on a tree. Through the work of Christ Jesus, God has blessed the Gentiles with the same blessing he promised to Abraham, and we Christians receive the promised Holy Spirit through faith." (Galatians 3:13–14)

A final word: Be strong with the Lord's mighty power. Put on all of God's armor so that you will be able to stand firm against all strategies and tricks of the Devil. For we are not fighting against people made of flesh and blood, but against the evil rulers and authorities of the unseen world, against those mighty powers of darkness who rule this world, and against wicked spirits in the heavenly realms. Use every piece of God's armor to resist the enemy in the time of evil, so that after the battle you will still be standing firm. Stand your ground, putting on the sturdy belt of truth and the body armor of God's righteousness. For shoes, put on the peace that comes from the Good News, so that you will be fully prepared. In every battle you will need faith as your shield to stop the fiery arrows aimed at you by Satan. Put on salvation as your helmet, and take the sword of the Spirit, which is the word of God. (Ephesians 6:10–17)

Don't worry about anything; instead, pray about everything. Tell God what you need, and thank him for all he has done. If you do this, you will experience God's peace, which is far more wonderful than the human mind can understand. His peace will guard your hearts and minds as you live in Christ Jesus. (Philippians 4:6–7)

For God has not given us a spirit of fear and timidity, but of power, love, and self-discipline. (2 Timothy 1:7)

Without wavering, let us hold tightly to the hope we say we have, for God can be trusted to keep his promise. (Hebrews 10:23)

Jesus Christ is the same yesterday, today, and for-ever. (Hebrews 13:8)

Are any among you sick? They should call for the elders of the church and have them pray over them, anointing them with oil in the name of the Lord. And their prayer offered in faith will heal the sick, and the Lord will make them well. And anyone who has committed sins will be forgiven. (James 5:14–15)

He personally carried away our sins in his own body on the cross so we can be dead to sin and live for what is right. You have been healed by his wounds. (1 Peter 2:24)

Dear friends, if our conscience is clear, we can come to God with bold confidence. And we will receive whatever we request because we obey him and do the things that please him. (1 John 3:21–22)

And we can be confident that he will listen to us whenever we ask him for anything in line with his will. And if we know he is listening when we make our request, we can be sure that he will give us what we ask for. (1 John 5:14–15)

A Letter from Heaven

Written by Donna Wright

Oh, Mom, I had to write and tell you how right you were about heaven. I opened my eyes to all that you told me about. The angels were singing all those songs that you so lovingly sang to me for years. I brought the words with me and I will be singing with all the angels.

I took all those hugs with me also, and my first hug to give out was to Jesus. I hugged him for you too, Mom, and told him how much you love him. Everything you said is true; Jesus really loves me. He spread his arms out wide and said, "Welcome to heaven, Haley, all this is for you."

Dad, we have the biggest park here, full of splendor and beauty, just like you always wanted me to enjoy. I did not know what to do first—run, jump or just touch each piece of beauty.

Jesus and I walked hand-in-hand; he touched a flower and I picked it for you, Mom. He also put a small pebble in my hand. We stood beside this beautiful glasslike pond just like the one I sat beside many times with Dad. I dropped the pebble into the pond, and the ripples grew, grew, and never ended. The unending ripples reminded me of your love and care for me. Thanks, Dad, for all that you did. Mom and Dad, thank you for loving me and telling me about Jesus. Jesus has been by my side for my first walk and talk. Mom, Dad, I am safe. I am healed. I am running. I am laughing. I am singing and I am looking forward to giving you this flower. Jesus said it is okay that I have already picked it, because in heaven everything is perfect and lives forever. I love you both.

From your perfect daughter.

CPSIA information can be obtained
at www.ICGtesting.com
Printed in the USA
JSHW041945140920
7839JS00005B/8

9 781098 035723